AM I SAFE?

Exploring Fear and Anxiety with Children

Includes a Discussion and Activity Guide and a special feature from singer/songwriter Steve Bell

BLESS YOU

WRITTEN BY IONA SNAIR AND TIM HUFF
ILLUSTRATED BY TIM HUFF

Published by:
Castle Quay Books
Burlington, Ontario
Tel: (416) 573-3249
E-mail: info@castlequaybooks.com | www.castlequaybooks.com

Edited by Marina Hofman Willard
Cover design and inside layout by Burst Impressions
Printed at Essence Printing, Belleville, Ontario

Library and Archives Canada Cataloguing in Publication

Huff, Tim, 1964-, author
      Am I safe? : exploring fear and anxiety with children / Tim Huff,
Iona Snair.

(Compassion series)
ISBN 978-1-988928-08-1 (EPUB)

      1. Anxiety--Juvenile literature. 2. Anxiety in children--Juvenile
literature. 3. Fear--Juvenile literature. 4. Fear in children--Juvenile
literature. 5. Courage--Juvenile literature. I. Snair, Iona, author
II. Title. III. Series: Compassion series

BF723.A5H84 2018   j155.4'1246   C2018-905114-0

DEAR GROWNUPS
A MESSAGE FROM IONA AND TIM

As you enter into this book, we want to both warmly welcome your good heart and share a bit about our hearts in creating it.

Together, we stepped into this project acutely aware of the complexities in tackling a subject with variables and nuances as unique as each precious child. The two of us have spent our entire adult lives immersed in career service among children and youth facing difficult realities. Perhaps even more significantly, we have also carried the fears and hurts of our own children within the contexts of our families. In both places we have experienced the uncertainty of not knowing what to do or say while longing desperately to make things better.

For parents, grandparents and teachers, we suspect that this feeling of uncertainty may be a familiar one. Our hope is that in this small book you may find one more piece of the many pieces that come together to help us walk well with the young ones who are dear to us. That journey requires that we acknowledge each child's unique experiences of the world and accept that what a child feels is real and sometimes horrible for them. Yet we must never forget that children have the capacity to learn to be in charge of difficult feelings rather than be controlled by them. We can guide our children to develop skills and tools for thriving and can cheer them on as they take steps small and large to flourish despite their difficulties. But all this takes an investment of time—time to model courage, choose compassion and bring hope. These things we can do.

We know only too well that the book title alone, Am I Safe?, may be a jarring question for anyone at any age or stage of life. This project is not meant to introduce a child to things worthy of their fear but rather to gently open the door for sharing about the named and unnamed concerns that lurk inside every child. Some of these are simply a part of childhood; others are a product of cultural realities; both need to be bravely acknowledged and expressed before children can find their way through them. In opening up this discussion, our desire is to bring a sense of courage in the middle of the uncertainties, rather than an empty promise of perfect safety. This is the honesty our children deserve.

Although written with the anxious or fearful child in mind, it is our hope that the book will provide all readers—children and grownups—with a window into the minds and hearts of the many in our world who are struggling with anxious feelings, opening the door for compassionate understanding as our response. The book has been uniquely designed with three distinct parts: an illustrated storybook for the children, a guide for the children and grownups to share, and finally a story just for the grownups. We suggest that the children's story is best initially read with adult and child together, offering time for the children to respond to the pictures and stanzas and discovering the places where the story intersects with their lives. Our hope is that children and grownups both will begin to believe that the journey from fear to courage is possible—in the book and for themselves.

From start to finish, we have purposed to write this book with great sensitivity toward our many differences, desiring to find a place where we can stand together—all faiths, cultures, family structures and educational paradigms. Our hope is that you will feel encouraged and equipped by our best efforts toward an end result that is equal parts truth, tenderness, insight, comfort and hope. But we would be remiss if we did not acknowledge that our shared heart in all of this comes predominantly from our faith in a loving God who cherishes the children in your care, just as he cherishes you. Our humble prayer is that the nearness and tenderness of ongoing discussions begun here result in immeasurable blessing for all of you.

Peace and joy to you and all those you cherish,
Iona and Tim

Am I safe? Am I okay?
Something's very wrong today!

Sometimes it feels like my "fear list" is long
With so many things in the world going wrong.
But fears are something everyone has—
Our teachers, our friends, our moms, and our dads.

For some people fears will pop up, then go;
For some, fears get stuck, and then start to grow.

For Katie, the fears come from uncertain thoughts—like wondering if she will be laughed at or not.

For Ella, the fears come from what she has seen—like when kids or adults are angry or mean.

For Jas, the fears come from what is NOT seen—like "what ifs" or "oh nos" that stick like bad dreams.

For Lucas, the fears keep wrapped up inside, then burst out as anger with nowhere to hide.

When fear comes to visit, its manners are poor.
It barges right in and kicks down the door.
Our stomachs get tight, our hearts start to race,
We can't fall asleep or feel safe any place.

When fear doesn't leave and decides it will stay,
It acts like a bully, scaring good things away.
We call this "anxiety"—it fills up our heads.
It spins thoughts around, causing worry and dread.

For me, I feel helpless—
alone in my fear.
"I'm sure something's wrong!"
is the whisper I hear.

The things that I want to do, now I just can't.
The fears are a giant—and I'm like an ant!

But WAIT! I'm still me, even though I feel small.
I'm strong and I'm brave—and I'm anxious, that's all.
There are things I can think and things I can say—
I'll find what I CAN do—and do it today.

The first thing I'll do is to name what I feel.
Then I'll look past the "what ifs" and see what is real.
I will start to talk back to the bully inside,
I'll breathe deep and remember I've no need to hide.

If you notice I'm anxious, please choose to come near.
If I seem kind of frozen, just know it's the fear.

This battle is real, but my weapons are strong.
Be kind, stand close by, and help me belong.

ABOUT THE GUIDE

The following pages are written for parents, grandparents and teachers. We hope they will place prompts and tools into your hands as you walk through Am I Safe? with the children in your care. It is meant to help you be a voice of comfort, perspective and hope.

 This icon marks the sections written to share with children, offering words that invite discovery and exploration of feelings in general and anxiety in particular.

 This icon marks the sections written specifically for the grownups, to equip you for this task with information, resources and activity ideas to lead you on the way.

PART 1: UNPACKING FEAR

Fear is a common experience of life that we all share. The aim of this section is to help children learn to be less afraid of fear and other uncomfortable emotions. Children who can acknowledge, identify and express the emotions they encounter are more likely to be able to manage those emotions rather than to be overwhelmed by them.

 ## NOTICE

The story begins with the words "Am I safe? Am I okay? *Something's very wrong today!*" Look at the faces of the children and the faces of the adults (page 5). What are some words that might describe how each of them are feeling?

 ## SHARE

This book talks about fear—fears about things that ARE happening and fears about things that MIGHT happen in our lives and the world around us. It reminds us that fear is simply one of the many emotions we have been given, and feeling fearful is something that everyone experiences at some point or another.

 ## READ

Sometimes it feels like my "fear list" is long
With so many things in the world going wrong.
But fears are something everyone has—
Our teachers, our friends, our moms, and our dads.

FYI

"Mean World Syndrome" is a fairly recent phenomenon affecting our society. The violent content of mass media (television, newspapers, print media, radio and the internet) convinces viewers that the world is more dangerous than it actually is. The viewer feels a desire for more protection than is warranted by the threat. Feelings of fear become predictors of danger instead of just feelings, keeping the individual on high alert at all times. Living with these beliefs is exhausting and spills into the lives of those around us!

The children in the first illustration (page 5) aren't watching the T.V.; they're watching the faces of their parents. Adults must be aware that their responses to fearful events in our world are deeply impactful to the children in their care. The following may provide some guidance as we manage our own fear:

- Tend to your own emotions in fearful times, finding your own safe places and safe people with whom to process them.
- Use wise discretion regarding what is age-appropriate and caution around oversharing with children.
- Guard against media saturation in your home.
- Remind children of all the ways they (and you) are safe.
- Validate children's feelings and share your own in gentle ways.
- Be your child's and family's safe place and calming voice.
- In times of hardship and tragedy focus early and often on the helpers and their courageous response.

DISCOVER

According to the dictionary, fear is the unpleasant feeling you have when you think that you're in danger.

Sometimes we think we're in danger and we're right!

Fear can warn us that a situation is unsafe and that something needs to be done, like stepping away from the edge of a slippery cliff, moving away from an angry dog or talking to a safe adult when we're being harmed by someone else.

When fear warns us of danger, it acts as a protector. This is what fear is meant to do. But it's not your only protector.

As a young person, you need to know that there are adults around you who take the job of keeping you safe very seriously. Some of these adults know you and some of them don't, but caring adults do all they can to keep you safe. This doesn't mean that they never feel afraid or that you won't still feel afraid at times, but it does mean that when fearful things come, you do not need to battle them alone.

EXPLORE

- Name one or two caring adults in your life who know you and do all they can to keep you safe.

• Make a list of the ways in which these caring adults in your life do all they can to keep you safe. (Encourage the young people to think of some specific actions of adults in different contexts, such as home, school, sports teams, police, faith communities and extended family.)

It's important to remember these caring adults so we know who we can talk to when we feel worried or unsafe.

FYI

The term "safe adult" can be hard to define, so here are five descriptive traits to help. (For older children, consider sharing these traits before asking them to name one or two "safe" adults.)

THOUGHTFUL: the person works at listening to you and believes you when you tell them something.
TRUSTWORTHY: the person can be depended upon to guard what you say and is someone you feel comfortable talking to.
RESPECTFUL: the person is mindful and considerate of your feelings and of your boundaries.
HELPFUL: the person provides guidance and helps you find solutions to problems.
CARING: the person does what's best for you, puts you first and cares about your mental and emotional well-being and physical safety.

(Adapted from kidshelpphone.ca)

SHARE

Talking to others about our fears can help us to feel less alone. It can also help us gain information or understanding about the thing we are afraid of. Sometimes that information helps us realize that our fear was based in not knowing all the facts, rather than based in true danger. Talking about fears can take courage because we aren't sure if others will understand or laugh at us, but we might be surprised how many people share the same fears we have.

ACTIVITY IDEA: FEARS IN A JAR

1. Label a number of containers (e.g., jars, bowls) with the name of a common childhood fear on each.
2. Leave one container blank and tell the children that the container represents fears that aren't written on the other containers.
3. Pass out 15 to 20 tokens (e.g., Lego pieces, bingo chips, puzzle pieces or buttons) to each child and invite them to join you in distributing their tokens among the containers based on which things they feel fear about and how much fear they feel about each. If one container represents a big fear for them, they can put most of their tokens in that container, or they can choose to divide their tokens between multiple containers.
4. Have the children place their tokens in the containers at the same time so that no one is singled out.
5. Once everyone is done, talk about how it feels to know you aren't the only one who has fears. Does it feel good to know you're not alone?

Here are some ideas for labels on the containers. (For a fuller list of common fears by age groups, visit www.compassionseries.com/amisafe.)

· Doing something embarrassing at school
· Bad people hurting me
· Being alone
· Family struggles
· People being mean to me
· Failing at school
· The dark
· Me or my family getting really sick or dying

FYI

It is a myth that inviting children to talk about their fears produces more fear. Fear already exists in every child—it's a normal part of life. Talking with children about their fears and providing them with information in a thoughtful and caring way actually reduce the confusion and shame that can accompany fears, opening the door for us to support children better. Of course, as adults we need to be wise about the kind of information we share with our children. Exposing them to fearful ideas or information that is beyond their context or experience is unwise, but discerning children's worries—based on what they have seen and heard—and talking to them about those things is a valuable and important part of helping them navigate the realities of their life.

TELL

Take this opportunity to tell a story from your own childhood of a fear that you sometimes had. It's important for children to know that even adults in authority were once children who felt like they do. Here's an example: "When I was young, if my mom or dad was late to pick me up, I would worry that something bad had happened. That was scary for me!"

READ

In our book we get a glimpse of four different children and the particular kinds of fears they battle (pages 8 and 9). Let's read about each child and see if we can relate to one of the four stories.

For Katie, the fears come from uncertain thoughts—like wondering if she will be laughed at or not.
For Ella, the fears come from what she has seen—like when kids or adults are angry or mean.
For Jas, the fears come from what is NOT seen—like "what ifs" or "oh nos" that stick like bad dreams.
For Lucas, the fears keep wrapped up inside, then burst out as anger with nowhere to hide.

What is happening in each picture (pages 8 and 9)? Look at the faces of the four children. How many emotions can you name that these children might be feeling?

 ## ACTIVITY IDEA: BIG BAD FEELINGS
(Recommended for family use)

Because feelings like fear are unpleasant and uncomfortable, many children become concerned that something is very wrong with them or the world when they experience these feelings. Some children confuse "uncomfortable" with "dangerous," and they try to avoid unpleasant feelings at any cost. Others can get lost in those unpleasant feelings, dwelling on them excessively. Both responses give difficult feelings too much power. Children need to recognize that unpleasant feelings are part of life, but they are places we visit, not places we need to live in. Acceptance of these feelings as a normal part of life opens up the door for a child to learn the skills they need to cope with their inner world rather than be overcome by it. Acceptance starts with recognition and identification of "what I feel."

1. Print (or draw together) a set of "BIG BAD FEELINGS" cards for each child and adult, listing unpleasant feelings we all experience, such as worried, lost, scared, ashamed, uncertain, nervous, sad or lonely. (For more examples of words and a printable card set with emojis, visit www.compassionseries.com/amisafe.)
2. Read through the words together and then take time individually to separate the cards into three piles—Never, Sometimes, Always—according to how often you experience that feeling. (Note: Tell the kids that if they don't know the meaning of a word they can put it aside.)
3. Invite the children to choose one of the feelings in the Always or Sometimes pile and tell one of the safe adults they named earlier about that feeling inside of them. If you're doing this activity with your own children or grandchildren, invite them to share those feelings with you. Safe adults care about what kids are feeling and listen to what they have to say.

"BIG BAD FEELINGS" cards can be used as an ongoing "feeling check" to aid in communication of emotions when a child is having a difficult day. They can be useful for helping children find the words to express what is going on inside and to share the difficult emotions rather than get lost in them.

 ## FYI
The act of putting a word or name on a feeling actually moves the experience of that emotion to a different part of the brain—the part that is more involved with solutions and actions. Generally speaking, when feelings are high, thinking is low. Putting a name on an emotion engages our brains, which begins to bring thinking up and feelings down. Doing this allows children to get "unstuck," moving them from being lost in a feeling to potentially engaging their minds in choosing what to do with the feeling.

EXPLORE

Show the children a balloon. Blow air into the balloon until it is about to burst.

Unpleasant feelings can be like air in a balloon. The more air that goes in, the more the balloon will be stretched and uncomfortable. It may even burst if none of the air is released!

Talking about feelings with a safe and caring person is like allowing the air to escape from the balloon (demonstrate by releasing some of the air). The balloon looks less stressed and stretched when some of the air is let out. Talking about our feelings makes us feel less stressed as well.

Remember that feelings, even the unpleasant ones like fear, are a normal part of life. They aren't bad, and they aren't dangerous. They are just uncomfortable, especially if we hold them all inside.

PART 2: FROM FEAR TO ANXIETY

Although fear is an experience common to all children, for some children fear takes over in a life-altering way for a time when anxiety takes root. Understanding how anxiety functions can help us extend greater empathy to children who suffer from its effects.

READ

For some people fears will pop up, then go;
For some, fears get stuck, and then start to grow.

DISCOVER

Remember our definition of fear? Fear is the unpleasant feeling you have when you think that you are in danger.

We've talked about the fact that sometimes we think we are in danger and we are right! When this happens, fear is doing what it is meant to do—it gives us a warning and helps us move away from dangerous things.

But sometimes we THINK we are in danger when we aren't. A scary thought about what COULD happen can cause our brains to yell "DANGER!"—just as if that thing really was happening—and a feeling of worry begins to grow. Worry affects our thoughts and our bodies and makes it hard to do the things that used to be easy.

For some people it's very difficult to make worry go away once it takes hold. When this occurs, fear moves from being a feeling caused by something on the outside to being an uninvited guest living on the inside.

FYI

Anxiety, stress and fear are not the same thing but often are present together. Childhood fears are common, and worry is definitely on the rise with young people, but anxiety takes the fear and worry and internalizes it at a deeper level. It stands in the way of children's ability to do things that they previously found easy or enjoyable. An anxiety disorder is a medical diagnosis for the impairment that anxiety creates. When anxiety resides within a child, the ongoing and significant distress can begin to define a child's life. Sometimes anxiety is triggered by an event or activity; but sometimes it simply hovers inside, bringing a general sense of unrest. Children with anxiety disorders are not always anxious about something; now they are simply anxious.

READ

Our book tells us about some of the ways fear or worry can act when it moves into our bodies. Here's what it says:

When fear comes to visit, its manners are poor.
It barges right in and kicks down the door.
Our stomachs get tight, our hearts start to race,
We can't fall asleep or feel safe any place.

ACTIVITY IDEA: BODY TALK

Most children have experienced worry and nervousness at some level, but not all children recognize that these emotions show themselves in our bodies, revealing what is going on before our minds have realized it. If children don't realize that their bodies are showing them how they feel, they can be concerned that something is very wrong with them, adding yet another worry to their list. When we help children recognize how worry or nervousness feels in their bodies, they can respond to the anxious feelings earlier, addressing them before they grow. We can reassure them that their bodies are working just as they were made to work and simply alerting them to what they are feeling.

Tell the children that you're going to explore some of the ways our bodies give us clues when we are experiencing worry or fear.

· Get each child to draw an outline of a body shape on a piece of paper. (Printable versions of this are available for download at www.compassionseries.com/amisafe.)
· List some examples of where worries and fear tend to show themselves while pointing to that spot on the body picture (racing heart, sweating, tight chest, fast breathing, clammy skin, red face, shaking or tense muscles, urge to cry, nausea, headache, stomach ache, fuzzy brain).
· Take a coloured marker and colour the places on the body picture where worry or fear shows itself in your body.
· Pass out markers or crayons and ask the children to colour areas on their body pictures that represent where nervousness or fear shows itself in them.

When our body responds to our feelings, we can simply say "Thank you for letting me know, body!" We can rest in knowing that our body is working just like it should—it just doesn't feel very good.

FYI

Because anxiety can feel so terrible, many who experience anxiety dread the POSSIBILITY of becoming anxious. Feeling anxious about getting anxious can become as debilitating as the original anxiety itself! Getting to know the warning signs of anxiety's approach allows a child to respond earlier with a plan to slow down the body and talk down the brain before anxiety fully takes over. Knowing the signs of anxiety can help a child feel less anxious about getting anxious—and more empowered to recognize and respond to what is going on in his or her body.

READ

When fear doesn't leave and decides it will stay,
It acts like a bully, scaring good things away.
We call this "anxiety"—it fills up our heads.
It spins thoughts around, causing worry and dread.

DISCOVER

It's time to learn two "A" words that both have to do with fear: Anxiety and Amygdala.

When fear or worry takes hold of our lives in a way that makes it hard to do everyday things like going to school, playing with friends or visiting new places, it is often called anxiety. Anxiety can be like a bully that keeps us from doing the things we want to do. It can make us feel like our brains aren't working properly, but the truth is that anxiety comes from a super-charged brain that is working overtime!

Adults: Prepare a noisemaker or alarm and keep it hidden from the children until this point. Suddenly engage the noisemaker or alarm with no warning. (Discern carefully what level of startling noise would be best for the children you are doing the activity with.) The loud noise will surprise the children and actually cause them to briefly experience the brain's fear response.

What happened in your body and brain when the sudden, unexpected sound surprised you? (Hint: They might not realize its effect on them. If so, be ready to point out what you felt in yourself and noticed in them. Most likely their hearts were racing, their bodies went on alert, their breathing sped up and hyperawareness kicked in.)

You have just met a part of your brain called the amygdala (a·myg·da·la)—and if you felt any reaction when you were surprised by the loud sound, then your amygdala is doing its job!

The amygdala is the part of the brain that is meant to warn us of danger. It has an important job, but sometimes the amygdala does its job too well! When that happens it starts acting like a smoke detector. A smoke detector is an important device that alerts us to trouble. But because it can't tell the difference between burnt toast and a house on fire, a smoke detector's alarm goes off for both as if one is as dangerous as the other. When the amygdala is overdoing its job, it's hard to figure out which things in life ARE dangerous and which things just FEEL dangerous. A super-charged amygdala responds to possibilities as if they were certainties. If I MIGHT get chased by a dog down the street, then when I think about walking past that yard a super-charged amygdala causes me to feel like I AM being chased!

Imagine going through every day wearing special glasses that show you every dreadful thing that could possibly go wrong. Now imagine feeling like these things are sure to happen! This would cause a feeling of dread inside about everyday things like going to school, playing with friends or going to sleep at night. When anxiety takes over, this is what the amygdala does, and it can feel overwhelming!

FYI

Anxiety is emotional rather than logical at its core. It may have begun with a fear based in a real event, but over time the person becomes unable to control that fear, despite little logical reason to worry. This is why trying to "talk someone out of" anxiety by telling them why they don't need to be worried is often ineffective. In fact, doing so may create greater anxiety because the child wonders why their brain isn't working as it should! Before we offer information, we need to listen, seeking to understand how it must feel to be in the child's shoes at that moment and letting them know that we are recognizing how dreadful they feel. When we accept and acknowledge anxious feelings, it does not make them worse. Rather, it begins to release children, because when they feel understood they can stop fretting about why they feel like they do and begin to move through the anxiety to the other side. Once their feelings are heard, we can offer them perspective and logic that they may have been missing, helping them to examine whether their fear is based in a true threat or an imagined one. When we are able to listen first, we communicate that we care about the person, not just about fixing the anxiety. It shows that we aren't panicking about their anxiety—so maybe they don't need to panic either.

READ

Our book introduces us to a boy named Eli. Eli is a real child just like you. Here's how he feels when the bully anxiety shows up in his life:

> For me, I feel helpless—alone in my fear.
> "I'm sure something's wrong!" is the whisper I hear.
> The things that I want to do, now I just can't.
> The fears are a giant—and I'm like an ant!

Look at the picture of the giant (page 13). What do you think he is saying to Eli? Will it be hard for Eli to stand up to the giant? Why? What do you think Eli should do? What would you do?

PART 3: FROM ANXIETY TO COURAGE

Anxiety is an incredibly disempowering emotion. An anxious child feels as if bad things are going to happen and they are powerless to do anything about it. All children are in need of courage at some point; the anxious child is in need of an extra measure of courage just to accomplish everyday tasks. The aims of this section are twofold: to empower and equip anxious children by giving them tools to address their anxiety and to introduce resources that any child—anxious or not—can use to process the difficult emotions they encounter.

READ

The good news is that once you can recognize anxiety, you realize that it's not as all-powerful as it seems. Children just like you are learning to stand up to the giant, calm the feeling of dread inside, and get back to living! That's the other part of Eli's story. Here's what he says:

> **But WAIT! I'm still me, even though I feel small.**
> **I'm strong and I'm brave—and I'm anxious, that's all.**
> **There are things I can think and things I can say—**
> **I'll find what I CAN do—and do it today.**
>
> **The first thing I'll do is to name what I feel.**
> **Then I'll look past the "what ifs" and see what is real.**
> **I will start to talk back to the bully inside,**
> **I'll breathe deep and remember I've no need to hide.**

EXPLORE

Eli learned some ways to walk THROUGH his anxiety rather than getting stuck IN it. With a lot of practice he was able to control his fears rather than his fears controlling him!

We're going to learn a few secrets for fighting back against scary big emotions like anxiety. Then you can take these ideas and begin to courageously use them—like your own personal superpowers—just like Eli did.

What things did Eli do to help him with his anxious feelings (page 15)? Have you ever tried any of these things? What things do you do when you feel small, worried or uncertain? What do you do to defeat anxious thoughts?

FYI

Increasing a child's repertoire of healthy coping skills builds resilience. Resilience is the ability to withstand and bounce back from the difficulties of life rather than being pulled under by them. The goal of resiliency is not to remove children from hard situations or to eliminate uncomfortable feelings, but rather to give them what they need to manage the situation without being consumed by it. Equipping children with tools to manage their anxiety empowers them and communicates that we believe they are strong enough to walk through difficult times. As a by-product of increased resiliency, anxiety will begin to diminish over time.

Because of our deep desire to not see children suffer, most of us have a natural tendency to try to rescue or "fix" rather than equip. When we step in and try to resolve their anxious feelings for them, it communicates that we believe they are too weak and need to be saved. It can be tricky to navigate our anxiety about their anxiety, but as adults we must walk alongside children rather than walk for them, helping them find and choose courageous things they can do to help themselves as we support and care for them. (For more resiliency-building ideas, visit www.compassionseries.com/amisafe.)

DISCOVER

One of the ways we become stronger is by exercising. There are some exercises you can learn that will help your courageous self to stand strong when big scary emotions come to call. Doing these things can actually keep your emotions from thinking they are in charge and remind your body that these are just feelings, and feelings always go away. (For more ideas, go to www.compassionseries.com/amisafe.)

• Grounding

When big scary emotions show up, it can feel like they are taking over our brains and we have no choice but to be overwhelmed by them. Big feelings tend to push clear thinking away, leaving us stuck with only the feelings. But we can learn to take back the control of our brains and stand up to those feelings! A good way to do that is to pull yourself away from the world inside of you where your feelings are in charge and step into the world that is in front of you—to "look past the 'what ifs' and see what is real." This is called "grounding." Here are a few ways you can "ground" yourself when big emotions threaten to fill you up:

1. **Find the Big Five:** Stop and ask and answer these five big questions to wake up your brain: What are five things I see? What are four things I can touch? What are three things I can hear? What are two things I smell? What is one thing I know?

2. **Make a List:** Choose a point ahead of you and work your way around the room, naming each thing that you see; or list all the boys' names or girls' names you can think of; or list all the gifts you gave and received last Christmas; or list as many things as you can think of that are red, blue or green. Come up with your own creative ideas of things you can list to distract and redirect your brain away from the anxious feelings.

3. **Take Notice:** Start at your toes and slowly work your way up your body—all the way to your eyebrows. Muscle by muscle, tense and then relax each one for the count of 10. Notice how it feels to be tense and how it feels to be relaxed.

4. **The Worry Jar:** Sometimes it can be hard to manage worrisome thoughts because they just keep coming back. Rather than allowing the thoughts to go around and around in circles, try creating a place for your worries to rest that is outside of your brain. Find a jar or other container and put papers and a pen next to it. When a worrisome thought keeps coming back, write it down on a paper and give the paper to the Worry Jar to hang on to for you so you don't have to. Then, on a specific day and time that you have chosen—for example, Mondays and Thursdays at 4:00 p.m.—you can read through the worries with a caring adult and decide what you need to do about them. If a worry returns after you have put it in the jar, remind yourself that it is already in the jar and will be cared for at the time you have chosen.

5. **Daily Dash:** Getting outside and playing a running or moving game provides more than just physical exercise. It tells your brain to send out calming "happy" chemicals called endorphins to your body. Make a chart for your wall that lists the days of the week with a checkbox next to each day. For every day that you do a Daily Dash activity for 30 minutes, mark 5 points on your chart. When you reach 50 points, reward yourself with a treat that you have chosen beforehand with your parents. You can get to 50 points even faster if a parent, sibling or friend joins you in the Daily Dash. Your daily points go up to 10 each time someone joins you. (And don't forget to share the treat with them at the end!)

6. **Mountain Breathing:** Everybody knows how to breathe, but most of us don't know how powerful our breath is. It can crush a giant—the fear giant—when it's done right! It takes practice to breathe deeply and slowly. It's especially hard when we are beginning to feel worried or nervous, but that is the BEST time to use this superpower.

   Start with pointing to the ground on one side of your body, and then slowly draw a tall mountain in the air. As you move up the mountain to the peak high above your head, breathe in without raising your shoulders (for about four counts). Then, slowly slide down the other side as you let all the air out (about four counts). See if you can climb the mountain five times. Can you feel your heartbeat slowing down? Can you feel your body relaxing?

   Practice doing this each day so that when you are feeling nervous or upset you will know how to breathe through it, up and down the tall mountain.

FYI

Deep breathing isn't a relaxation trick; its positive effects are a physiological fact. It decreases blood pressure, lowers heart rate, increases the oxygen in the bloodstream and stirs up the kind of brain waves that are present in a relaxed state. Breathing deeply and slowly changes our body state and essentially tells anxiety to "stand down!" To be most effective, deep breathing needs to be learned and practised BEFORE anxiety is present. This allows the body to go to a memorized place when anxiety is making it difficult to think, choose and move. Teaching the body to rest—whether by practising breathing techniques or enforcing regular, healthy amounts of sleep—helps the body to be in the strongest position possible for battling anxious feelings when they come.

ACTIVITY IDEA: COURAGE KITS

Invite the children to brainstorm a list of ideas for managing unpleasant feelings. Ask what has worked for them in the past and what they can imagine will be helpful in the future. Have the children select three or four things from the list that fit for them—things they could do in the face of difficulty. Then help them choose a small creative reminder or symbol of each of those practices. Each child's collection of ideas can be stored in any small, portable and accessible container, such as a small dollar store box that fits in a backpack, an envelope that tucks in a binder, a pouch that can be worn around the neck or a change purse for their pocket.

Here are a few ideas for a courage kit:

· A song, verse or picture that is particularly comforting
· An item from a place or time where being strong and courageous was experienced (e.g., a smooth stone picked up at camp)
· A soft fabric for tactile comfort
· A picture or phone number of a comforting person to remind them that they aren't alone
· Names of people they know who are also struggling (to remind them that they aren't the only ones)
· A funny picture linked to a good memory
· A card with drawn symbols of "the big five" (see sample at www.compassionseries.com/amisafe)
· A picture of a mountain to remind them to use "mountain breathing"

PART 4: FROM COURAGE TO COMPASSION

This final section calls children to take their courage and use it to offer compassion expressed through presence. Our aim is that children recognize that they have something to contribute when they encounter others who are struggling along the way.

FYI

Courage means

· the ability to do something that frightens you
· strength in the face of pain or grief

Courage is not the absence of fear but the choice to move forward despite fear.

Compassion means

· "Com"—with or together
· "Passion"—to endure or suffer

Compassion is enduring together so we can thrive together.

SHARE

We've discovered that there are many unpleasant feelings in the world, and every one of us has experienced at least one of them at some point. Together we explored what it feels like to be nervous or worried about fearful things and what some children experience when anxiety moves in and holds them back from living a full life for a while. Naming and sharing our feelings with caring adults and friends can make those feelings a little less scary, and learning how to be in charge of our bodies and minds can help us walk through anxious or difficult times rather than getting stuck in them. We don't need to be afraid of fear, and feelings of fear don't need to bully us into missing out on life! If anxious times come, it helps to know that (1) we aren't alone, (2) the feelings are uncomfortable but not dangerous, and (3) when they pass we will see that we are strong and can even stand with others who are having difficulties. Together we can learn that courage isn't shown by never being afraid; it is shown by learning and choosing to do strong and good things for ourselves and for others when fear and anxiety come.

ACTIVITY IDEA: FEELING UNDERSTOOD

Through the following activity, children experience the frustration of not being understood by others, as well as the relief of being understood. When we are understood, suddenly we no longer feel alone.

1. Lead the children in playing a short game of Pictionary or charades together.
2. Talk about how it felt to not be understood versus how it felt to be understood. Was it a relief to have the time run out so you could just use your words? When someone guessed correctly, how did you feel toward them?

After the game and conversation, tell the children that when others around us experience difficult or unpleasant emotions like anxiety, they can feel like no one understands. That can feel lonely and frustrating, especially when it seems like others don't notice.

DISCOVER

Ask the children to close their eyes and try to imagine how others might feel if

· They weren't invited to a friend's birthday party.
· They got yelled at in front of the whole class.
· They lost their favourite toy or game.
· They were the only one who forgot there was a test today.

Imagining what it's like to step into someone else's shoes helps us understand others a bit more. This is called EMPATHY. Empathy is the ability to recognize and care about how a situation is making someone else feel. It doesn't always come naturally, but the more we practice, the better we get at it. When you notice that someone is having a hard time, you are feeling empathy; when you take time to let them know you understand, then you are practising empathy. Empathy is the beginning of compassion.

· What are some things you could do or say to let your friend who is having a hard time know that you have noticed and that you care?

READ

Eli gives us an idea about one simple thing we can do when we realize a friend is feeling anxious. But he also reminds us that we don't need to feel or "battle" anxiety for our friends. We just need to let them know they are not alone:

> **If you notice I'm anxious, please choose to come near.**
> **If I seem kind of frozen, just know it's the fear.**
>
> **This battle is real, but my weapons are strong.**
> **Be kind, stand close by, and help me belong.**

TELL

For some adults there are songs and poems and prayers that have touched their lives during fearful and anxious times. Reflecting on the ones you recall that impacted you when you were around the age of the children in your care and sharing them as you are able can provide wonderfully special moments of comfort and care.

SHARE

As we end our journey together, we wanted to offer the sweet gift of song. "A Heartbeat Away" was written especially for this book by Canadian singer-songwriter Steve Bell. We invite you to download the song for free at www.compassionseries.com/heartbeat and share the gentle message of the song together.

This song is your song now. Carry it in your mind and heart, and share it with others who might be in need of the compassion you have to offer.

A FINAL WORD

Our final word brings us right back to where we started in the Dear Grownups message: nearness and tenderness are invaluable. They can be complemented with helpful information and important insights but not replaced by them. We may not always know the words to say or things to do, but standing close by is always where we need to begin.

ELI'S STORY FOR THE GROWNUPS

*S*hortly after my first book for adults, Bent Hope, was released in 2008, I invited a number of my most respected and talented friends to contribute thoughts and essays on the subject of hope as part of a blog series. Of course, Iona was at the top of that list. That she was a trusted long-time friend was a great bonus, but I reached out knowing only too well of her incredible history of service among broken-hearted young people, her gifting as a mentor to young social-justice leaders and her exceptional teaching and writing skills. I was happily surprised when she asked if she could take my request in a very different direction and tackle the issue of hope by way of a transparent interview with her young son, addressing his challenges with anxiety. Eli, now a vibrant young man, has graciously agreed to have this piece shared a second time as part of this published work. What a gift it is to share that lovely and brave interview as part of Am I *S*afe?!

This is a glimpse of one family's story—about lessons learned and challenges embraced. It provides a window into the reality that the journey through anxiety seldom involves a "quick fix," yet that is what most parents would deeply desire in the quest to keep their children from feeling unsafe. But maybe true safety is better found in the possession of courage rather than the absence of pain. As we stand well with our anxious children they can begin to believe that they are strong and they are able and they CAN stand for themselves in the face of anxious feelings.

STAND CLOSE BY

When anxiety came to our house, it didn't come inconveniently, like an uninvited guest—it came violently and unimaginably, like a home invasion. Our son Eli was nine years old—an explorer and adventurer, with an unstoppable drive to conquer every inch of the forest behind our house and populate it with the legends he and his buddies would fashion from bits and pieces of the stories they loved. Terabithia was back there; Narnia came and went; Mordor of Tolkien's Middle Earth cloaked the simple birch and cedars with captivating menace and mystery every day.

It happened so quickly that we missed all the signs and found ourselves quite suddenly immersed in a new world. This one had none of the enchanting fairy-tale elements that had entranced our boy in the past. This one had only the darkness and dragons—and a young knight caught unaware and unprepared for the battle ahead. From Eli's perspective, here's how it felt to be plummeted into this new place:

> I remember what it was like when the anxiety started. It felt sick. It felt bad. It felt horrible. I kept thinking something was going to happen even though they said it wasn't. *Something is going to happen to my mom. Something bad is going to happen to me.* The thoughts went over and over in circles in my head. I pictured death, destruction, sadness. The things I feared might happen were in my head all the time, and even though it made things worse I just couldn't stop picturing them. I would try to tell myself to stop, but then something small would happen—like a thought or someone being late or even a noise—and my thoughts would go back to thinking about all the bad things that I was sure were going to happen to me and my family.
>
> Nothing seemed to work to make it go away. Even if it worked for a while, the thoughts would come back. The thoughts made me want to throw up. I just wanted it to stop—it made me want to disappear so I could make it stop. I knew nothing bad was really happening, but thinking about it was like it was true. It was horrible. I couldn't stop my thoughts. And then when something I feared would happen did happen—like I'd get separated from my mom in a crowd—I regretted over and over doing whatever I had done to get into that spot and told myself I needed to make sure that it never happened again. I felt fear, sadness and hopelessness, and the feelings wouldn't go away.

We've learned a lot about anxiety since those early days. We've learned that our son has an anxiety disorder that may reside in him for life. We've learned that, for him, the fear has very little to do with what is happening externally and much to do with his internal pictures of what might happen; he responds to the potential for pain as if it were actual pain. The same imagination that took him on his many adventures now serves to create a world that feels unsafe and uncertain. The same sensitivity that caused him to instinctively know how others were feeling and to meet the world with gentleness and compassion now leaves him overwhelmed and emotionally exhausted.

In the first year after the anxiety took hold we tried deep breathing, self-talk, medication, diet change, support groups and skill building, but Eli remained very fragile. Crowds and chaos could trigger anxiety, but so could sitting alone and thinking.

> I wanted all the things my parents were trying to get me to do to work, but they just didn't seem to help. I felt like there was nothing that could be done that would work. I felt like I couldn't beat it—like I was going to be stuck like this forever. I met another kid who was really anxious, but I was afraid to talk to him because I thought he might feel different than me and just think I was weird. Sometimes I still feel like nobody could understand me and I need someone to talk to who feels the same way as I do. I wonder if anybody feels the same as me.

Eli wasn't the only one feeling overwhelmed. As his mom, I just wanted to make it better and correct all his faulty perceptions so they wouldn't have power over him. It's not as simple as that. I remember one night sitting by the window during a neighbourhood power outage and looking out at the darkness with Eli. I could almost feel his anxiety mounting, and he said, "Mom, I feel like everyone has disappeared and we're the only ones left alive. I know that's not true, but I'm really really scared."

I responded, "Of course it's not true. It's just a storm—no big deal. There's nothing to worry about. Everything is fine." The words tripped over each other, rushing out of my mouth. The information was true and accurate, but before Eli could hope to hear it he needed to have me hear and acknowledge what was happening inside him—to stand with him in the very real fear he was experiencing. In my panic over his growing anxiety I tried to rescue him with accuracy, when I could have stepped into his shoes, stood with him there for a minute and said, "Honey, it must feel so scary to think that might be true. Those are really big feelings. What do you think you're going to need to do to get through to the other side of this horrible feeling?"

It took some time, but we began to learn that what Eli needed most wasn't to have us "fix" his feelings; he needed to know that in the middle of his anxious thoughts he was not alone, he was strong, and he could make it through. In the beginning, my protective instinct was to make him feel safe by rushing to set his thoughts straight. But soon I realized that my best efforts to redirect and reassure didn't seem to have any lasting effect if I wasn't willing to first take the time to calmly face the reality of his feelings with him. My desire to rescue my son actually served to create a dependency on me—and a feeling that he really was powerless to stand.

But he was not powerless. And he was not standing alone.

Over time, we walked with Eli as he discovered the things he could do to manage and reduce the anxiety. He created a "courage kit" that he carried in a small pouch around his neck with reminders of things he could do when the anxious feelings began to percolate within him. Because of our family's faith, some of those things were reminders that God was standing with him. And some were reminders that he could stand with others. One item in the kit was a list of four people he knew who also battled anxiety. The list reminded him to pray for them when anxiety struck him.

> That really helped, because I realized I wasn't the only one in the world feeling this way. Praying for them got my mind off myself and actually helped me feel better because I realized that a lot of people are fighting the same things I'm fighting—and maybe if I stand with them they'll be stronger. And maybe I will be too.

I remember back to when Eli was in kindergarten. One day at dinner he was telling us about how sometimes kids got hurt on the playground and it really disturbed him. We asked, "What do you do when that happens?"

"Well," he said, "I don't really know what to do, so I just go over and stand close by them while they're crying until help comes."

Eli figured out something that some of us take a lifetime to grasp. Sometimes there is no quick fix; sometimes there is no easy answer. It just hurts. And what we need most is someone to stand close by. It doesn't make the pain go away, but it makes it possible to bear.

The anxiety isn't gone, but together we're continuing to learn what it looks like to stand close and share the difficult days without having them define our lives. The invader no longer has control of our home, and at times we dare to believe that life is "back to normal." But then anxiety returns and we realize that, for now, perhaps this is our normal. And if standing together means standing here for a while, then it's where we need to be.

AUTHORS' ACKNOWLEDGEMENTS

We are both profoundly thankful for the never-ending support we've received on this project, and through all of life's adventures, from our precious families. You are adored beyond words.

To our priceless friends—too many to thank by name in this small space—know that each of us will always strive to do our best in our day-to-day lives to ensure you know how much we appreciate you.

Referencing this project specifically, with great gratitude we want to acknowledge the goodness of Terri and Miller Alloway, Patrick Boller, Greg Paul, Kelly and Brad Pedersen, Kym and the Lukin children, Nicky Wilson, the ever-faithful members of the Compassion Series Council, and the gracious Signpost Music family. And certainly, great and humble thanks to Eli for freely sharing his important story.

Special thanks to Julia Beazley and Annie Brandner for invaluable input and review work, and to Cindy Thompson for all of the excellent layout and design work.

Special thanks to Jeff Lukin for kindly providing ideal background photos to complement many of the illustrated pages.

And, of course, we also share in great and many thanks to Larry and Marina Willard and the Castle Quay Books family for believing in and supporting this meaningful project.

To our sisters and brothers at Youth Unlimited chapters in Toronto and Vancouver and the Lifeteams family—thank you for your faithful support and encouragement. And to our dear friends and associates from YU chapters across Canada and at the YU (YFC) National office, be assured of our admiration and thanksgiving for your inspiration and kinship.

And we would be remiss not to enthusiastically thank all the gracious supporters who have come alongside our many social justice and community building endeavours through Youth Unlimited over a great many years, in a great many ways. Know always that your faithful generosity and care are vital and ever-appreciated.

A GIFT FROM STEVE BELL:
"A HEARTBEAT AWAY"

Both Iona and I have known and admired Steve Bell for most of our adult lives. Steve was a dear co-worker with Iona many years ago in Winnipeg and, by way of many shared projects and travels, has come to be one of my most trusted and faithful friends.

While various versions of the Am I Safe? project had been swirling in my head since 9/11, it was years later on the drive to one of Steve's concerts—while listening to the terrible news of the Sandy Hook school shootings on the radio—that I promised myself I'd somehow find a way to make it happen. After Steve's concert that night I told him that I had this long-range plan for an Am I Safe? children's book and that I really felt it needed a special song to go with it. At the time, I envisioned what I called a "family lullaby." Without hesitation, Steve agreed to take it on. It was several years later, having sorted out a working plan with Iona and Castle Quay Books, when I circled back to my conversation with Steve.

Steve Bell is truly one of Canada's great treasures. An internationally acclaimed, multi-award-winning singer-songwriter, Steve has more than 20 beautiful albums to his name. Moreover, Steve is a gifted musician, speaker and writer who is rooted in a deep faith and driven by the purest notions of compassion, justice, peace and goodness. On this special project Steve was blessed with the gift of contribution from his daughter-in-law, singer-songwriter Diana Pops.

We are thrilled to share this song with you as a sweet gift, a humble commission honoured and a very significant element of the Am I Safe? project. May you and those you cherish be greatly blessed by "A Heartbeat Away."

Download "A Heartbeat Away" for free at
www.compassionseries.com/heartbeat

For more about Steve Bell and his music visit
www.stevebell.com

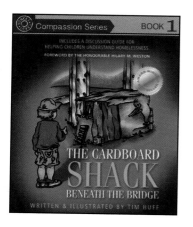

COMPASSION SERIES BOOKS FOR CHILDREN

**The Cardboard Shack Beneath the Bridge:
Helping Children Understand Homelessness**
Written and Illustrated by Tim Huff
Foreword by The Honourable Hilary M. Weston

It's Hard Not to Stare: Helping Children Understand Disabilities
Written and Illustrated by Tim Huff
Discussion Guide by Jan Fukumoto
Foreword by The Honourable David C. Onley

The Honour Drum: Sharing the Beauty of Canada's Indigenous People with Children, Families and Classrooms
Written by Cheryl Bear (Nadleh Whut'en First Nation, BC) and Tim Huff
Discussion Guide by Cheryl Bear
Illustrated by Tim Huff
Forewords by Ray Aldred (Cree) and Steve Bell

BOOKS FOR ADULTS AND TEENAGERS (16+)

Bent Hope: A Street Journal
Written by Tim Huff
Foreword by Michael Frost, Benediction by Steve Bell

Dancing With Dynamite: Celebrating Against the Odds
Written by Tim Huff
Foreword by Jean Vanier, Benediction by Sue Mosteller, C.S.J.

The Yuletide Factor: Cause for Perpetual Comfort and Joy
Written by Tim Huff
Reflection and Discussion Guide by Anne Brandner
Interludes by Steve Bell and Greg Paul
Foreword by Moira Brown, Benediction by Lorna Dueck

All of Tim Huff's titles have been published by Castle Quay Books and are available at www.castlequaybooks.com/timhuff.

For book overviews, news on upcoming titles and book related events, and purchase information visit www.compassionseries.com/books.

Current and future audio book versions of Tim Huff titles are produced by Talking Book Library (www.talkingbooklibrary.org**) in partnership with Castle Quay Books.**

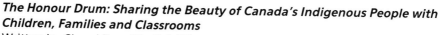